SCOOBY-DOO!

and the Truth Behind
GHOSTS

BY TERRY COLLINS

ILLUSTRATED BY CHRISTIAN CORNIA

CAPSTONE PRESS
a capstone imprint

Published in 2015 by Capstone Press,
A Capstone Imprint
1710 Roe Crest Drive
North Mankato, Minnesota 56003
www.capstonepub.com

CAPS33178

Library of Congress Cataloging-in-Publication Data
Collins, Terry (Terry Lee), author.
Scooby-Doo! and the truth behind ghosts /
by Terry Collins ; illustrated by Christian Cornia.
pages cm. —— (Unmasking monsters with Scooby-Doo!)
Summary: "The popular Scooby-Doo! and the Mystery Inc. gang
teach kids all about ghosts"—— Provided
by publisher.
Audience: Ages 6-8.
Audience: K to grade 3.
Includes bibliographical references and index.
ISBN 978-1-4914-1791-1 (library binding)
1. Ghosts—Juvenile literature. 2. Curiosities and wonders—
Juvenile literature. I. Cornia, Christian, 1975– illustrator. II.
Title. III. Title: Ghosts.
GR580.C644 2015
133.1—dc23   2014029119

Editorial Credits:
Editor: Shelly Lyons
Designer: Ted Williams
Art Director: Nathan Gassman
Production Specialist: Tori Abraham

Design Elements:
Shutterstock: ailin1, AllAnd, hugolacasse, Studiojumpee

The illustrations in this book were created traditionally, with
digital coloring.

Thanks to our adviser for her expertise, research, and advice:
Elizabeth Tucker Gould, Professor of English
Binghamton University

Printed in the United States of America in
Stevens Point, Wisconsin
092014   008479WZS15

"Like, whose idea was it to spend the night in Baron Creepy's house again?" Shaggy asked.

"Act cool, team," said Fred. "The TV producers of *Ghost Grabbers* asked for us specifically."

"That's what worries me," Shaggy whispered.

"Shh!" Daphne hissed. "My microphone is picking up a spooky sound!"

"I'll tape it with the recorder," Velma said. "Fred, can you get closer with the video camera?"

"Where is Scooby?" Shaggy asked. "Oh, no! The ghost must have grabbed him!"

The sound is coming from that suit of armor, Velma said.

As the gang watched, the visor of the helmet flipped open to reveal the face of Scooby-Doo!

"Boo!" barked Scooby.

Velma played back the recording. "GRRROWL!"

"Hey, that's not a ghost!" Daphne cried. "That's Scooby's stomach growling!"

"Like, who says ghosts really exist anyway?" asked Shaggy.

"Scientists say there are no ghosts, because there's no proof," Velma said. "But witnesses say otherwise."

"That's right," Fred added. "Paranormal investigators have heard strange sounds. They've also taken photos and videos that can't be explained."

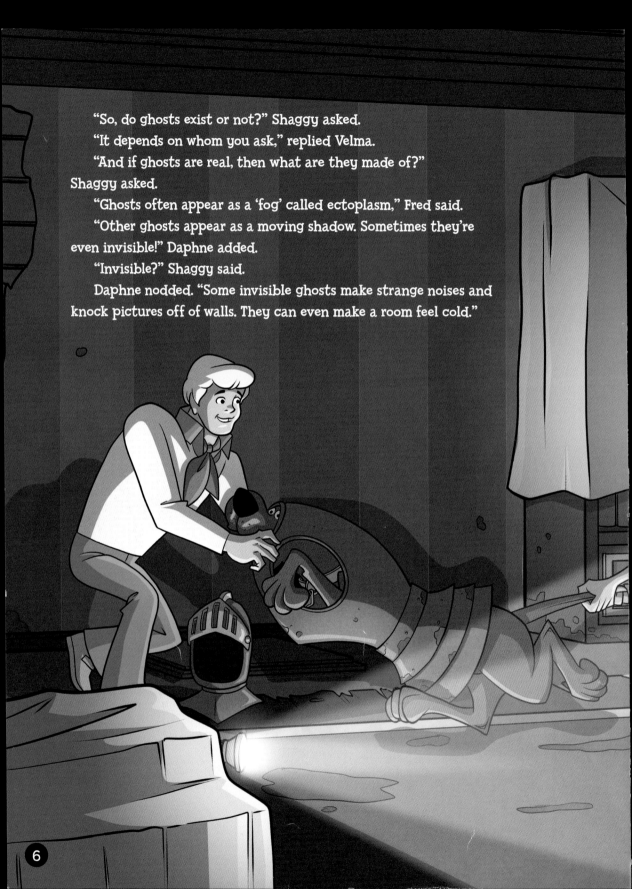

"So, do ghosts exist or not?" Shaggy asked.

"It depends on whom you ask," replied Velma.

"And if ghosts are real, then what are they made of?" Shaggy asked.

"Ghosts often appear as a 'fog' called ectoplasm," Fred said.

"Other ghosts appear as a moving shadow. Sometimes they're even invisible!" Daphne added.

"Invisible?" Shaggy said.

Daphne nodded. "Some invisible ghosts make strange noises and knock pictures off of walls. They can even make a room feel cold."

"Zoinks! Run, Scoob!" Shaggy cried.

"Relax, Shaggy," Daphne said. "That's just your helmet light reflecting in the mirror."

"It looked like a ghost orb," Velma offered.

"What's a ghost orb?" Shaggy asked.

"It's a ball of light that often mysteriously appears in pictures," Fred answered. "Some people think these orbs might be ghostly spirits."

"Most orbs are really a camera's flash reflecting off dust particles in the air," Velma said. "But eyewitnesses have reported seeing orbs when the photos were taken."

"Just us!" Shaggy replied, "We ran into the china cabinet."

"I thought the noise might have been a poltergeist," Velma said.

"What's a poltergeist?" Shaggy asked.

"It's a ghost that's heard but not seen. They make loud noises and hide things like a person's keys, " said Fred. "Sometimes an angry poltergeist even breaks dishes or other items."

"Remind me to stay away from poltergeists," Shaggy muttered.

"Reah!" Scooby agreed.

"Do ghosts haunt ships too?" Shaggy asked.

"Sure, the *Flying Dutchman* is thought to be a cursed ghost ship," Daphne replied.

"Rying Rutchman?" Scooby barked.

"It sails the world, haunting sailors in the black of night," Daphne explained.

"The *Flying Dutchman*'s crew of spirits is doomed to roam the oceans forever," Velma added. "According to legend seeing the ship is considered bad luck."

"Maybe we should stick to ghost hunting on dry land," Shaggy suggested.

"Do we have everything needed to find a ghost?" Shaggy asked.

"People use lots of different tools to find a ghost," Velma added. "We have the basics with us, but there are many useful tools."

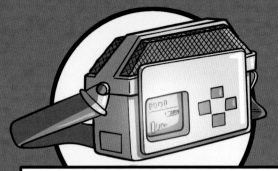

DIGITAL AUDIO RECORDER AND MICROPHONES

DIGITAL VIDEO CAMERA

DIGITAL STILL CAMERA WITH INFRARED CAPABILITIES

NIGHT VISION GOGGLES

MOTION DETECTOR

ELECTROMAGNETIC FIELD (EMF) METER

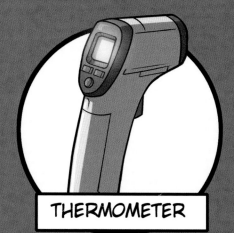

THERMOMETER

"Are there any ghosts of famous people?" Shaggy asked.

"Of course," Fred replied. "The ghost of the famous musician Elvis Presley is said to haunt Graceland. Graceland was his mansion in Memphis, Tennessee."

"Visitors to the White House say they have seen the ghost of former U.S. president Abraham Lincoln walking the halls," Daphne said.

"Like, if I saw one of those ghosts, I wouldn't know whether to run or ask for an autograph!" Shaggy joked.

So much for our television debut," Shaggy said. "We're back where we started from and still no ghosts!"

"Oh, I wouldn't say that," Fred said. "Check behind you."

"Raggy!" Scooby said. "Rook!"

"H-h-haunted knight!" Shaggy cried. "Gangway!"

"Oh, well. *Ghost Grabbers* can always use this footage for a comedy," Daphne laughed.

GLOSSARY

ectoplasm—a "fog" said to produce a spirit

electronic voice phenomena (EVP)—sounds heard on recordings that were not heard when originally recorded; some say EVP is the sound of ghosts

paranormal investigator—someone who studies events that science can't explain

poltergeist—a noisy ghost that sometimes moves, hides, or breaks things

READ MORE

Martin, Michael. *The Unsolved Mystery of Ghosts*. Unexplained Mysteries. North Mankato, Minn.: Capstone Press, 2013.

Perish, Patrick. *Are Haunted Houses Real?* Unexplained: What's the Evidence? Mankato, Minn.: Amicus High Interest, 2014.

INTERNET SITES

FactHound offers a safe, fun way to find Internet sites related to this book. All of the sites on FactHound have been researched by our staff.

Here's all you do:

Visit *www.facthound.com*

Type in this code: 9781491417911

 **Super-cool stuff!** Check out projects, games and lots more at **www.capstonekids.com**

INDEX